# Tea & Teardrops

How we survived the bad times

www.shoehornbooks.com

Shoehorn Arts & Culture Books

Published by
Shoehorn Media Ltd
4 Great Marlborough Street
London W1F 7HH
England

www.shoehornbooks.com

A CIP catalogue record for this book is available from the British Library.

ISBNs: 978 1 907149 12 2 (hardback) 978 1 907149 13 9 (softback)

Printed in the UK by LSUK, Milton Keynes.

# Contents

# Foreword

**Jonathan Welfare**
Chief Executive, Elizabeth Finn Care

Ever since The Distressed Gentlefolk Aid Association, now known as Elizabeth Finn Care, was established in 1897, we have been providing help and support to those who find themselves in financial difficulty. Times may have changed; however, the reasons people suffer financial hardship haven't, be it family breakdown, redundancy or illness.

This book tells the very personal stories of some household names, and of those relating directly to individuals who we are currently helping, or those that we have supported through a difficult time and are now "back on their feet". What stands out is the strength of character displayed by all these people, and a determination not be beaten. Each story is inspirational in its own way, and each has a lesson for all of us. Lynda Bellingham says: "It all seemed to happen at once." Elizabeth Finn Care hears these words time and time again, as events tend to unfold so quickly leaving people unable to cope. Bellingham also tells of an emotional blackness, and it can be that feeling of emptiness that people find the hardest to deal with. But the mere fact there is someone on the end of a telephone ready to listen and able to start you on the road to recovery can make all the difference in the world.

Simon Weston's story from the Falklands War is familiar to us all, but hearing it again does nothing to weaken our sense of admiration for a man faced by unfathomable difficulties. The support given by teams of dedicated professionals can act as a spur to those in need.

The charity's name may have changed, but our role is exactly the same as it was at the end of the 19th century – to provide non-judgemental help to those that need it. We pride ourselves on helping people back onto their feet, back to work and back into society. Even now, in a recession, we continue to grow and adapt to the changing world around us. Elizabeth Finn Care has the very same fortitude and determination to overcome the odds as that displayed by the people you will read about here.

## Perry Fenwick

# "When you've no job, the last thing you want to do is be dwelling on it all the time, but the isolation that comes with having no money means you don't really have a choice."

Perry Fenwick has played Billy Mitchell in Britain's most popular soap, *EastEnders*, for the last eleven years. His first regular TV role was in *Watching*, but he has also appeared in *Inspector Morse*, *The Brittas Empire* and *Minder*, whilst film roles include cult classic, *I.D.* as well as *The Winslow Boy* and *Mona Lisa*.

Given what I do for a living, I'm used to up and downs. It goes without saying that acting is a rocky profession and one – and I can't believe I'm saying this – that I've been working in for over thirty-years.

My first few acting gigs were at the back of the pantomime horse. But pantomime horse quickly evolved into *Peter Pan* and within a very short space of time, I was soaring up the

ladder. I was a kid back then, so it didn't occur to me that I was lucky, at least not until much later and when all of a sudden things weren't looking so rosy.

Within a couple of years of starting out, I was getting lead parts and I just thought that was how it happened. Then, towards the end of the 1980s, it just stopped – suddenly and without warning. I couldn't get arrested, let alone get a part.

All I had to show from those early years was a little flat I'd bought myself in east London; my own little corner of the world. Although things were bad – with the taxman snapping at my heels and what not – I still had my nest and it gave me a bit of dignity at the end of the day.

# 🫖 Perry Fenwick

One day I noticed a little crack in the living room wall. One crack very quickly turned into half a dozen. I scraped some money together to get someone to come and have a look and it was confirmed to be subsidence. What an awful time! There I was, jobless and flat broke. That one little investment that had given me some self-respect was now – like me – literally sinking.

I couldn't sell; no one would want to buy. I couldn't get it fixed; there was no money to pay for it. After that, things just went from bad to worse emotionally.

It didn't help that I could barely afford a proper meal, let alone go out and meet up with mates. When you've no job, the last thing you want to do is be dwelling on it all the time, but the isolation that comes with having no money means you don't really have a choice.

Another problem with the acting game is that you're not selling a trade as such. It's not like being a carpenter, where you build some shelves and what not. An actor has to sell *themselves* and when your confidence has taken a massive knock, it's hard to make a good job of that. The more rejections you get, the more your self-esteem takes a whack, and so it just becomes this vicious circle.

I actually got panicky then about acting again, which was just terrible because if I couldn't even call myself an actor, I really did feel like I had nothing. It was a really black time for me. I didn't want get out of bed, I couldn't see what the point of anything was and even stopped picking up the phone.

But then one day I received something through the post and things changed. It was from Mum, who wasn't exactly well off herself. I can't remember what newspaper it was, but one of the tabloids was offering a deal. Something along the lines of, if you collect five tokens over five days, you get a free meal at McDonalds.

It sounds stupid, but it was the way she had put it all together. She'd cut the vouchers out so meticulously and attached with paperclips to the card. It was only a free feed, but it touched me so much. For whatever reason, it was the wake-up call I needed. I'm lucky in that I'm the kind of person that can't feel sorry for themselves for too long. It really made me access things and say, "Do you know what, Perry? You've got two arms and two legs and you're going to be just fine. It's just a lull, things aren't that bad."

After that, I *made* myself get out of bed and go to auditions. If I wasn't feeling confident, I pretended I was. Being an actor, that's what it's about at the end of the day, anyway. When I got a job, it was a giant leap out of what was a very difficult time.

It's taught me that what you put out, you get back. If you walk around all the time with a black cloud over you, you're going to attract like for like. I'm stronger and less inclined to feel sorry for myself these days. It just shows how much a little help from someone who cares can go a very long way. If I'm ever having a down day or whatever, even now I look back at Mum's card and it really does give me hope and a sense of perspective.

## Cliff Morgan

# "There was little money but there was always food on the table."

**Cliff Morgan is a former Welsh rugby union player who played for Cardiff RFC and earned 29 caps for Wales between 1951 and 1958. Following his retirement from the game he found a new career in broadcasting and supervised coverage of the biggest broadcast events such as football World Cups, Commonwealth and Olympic Games, as well as royal weddings and other national ceremonial occasions.**

I am a man from the Rhondda, son of a miner, who was blessed to have a mother and father who cared. It was, without doubt, my parents who gave me the foundations which allowed me to relish a wonderful life through rugby and broadcasting. Our home was all about love and faith, caring and discipline. Brought up in the small village of Trebanog, I had an idyllic childhood. There was little money but there was always food on the table – wonderful home cooking – and a welcoming home though with no bath, no central heating and an outside lavatory!

From a young age I went with my parents to chapel every Sunday, joined them in the choir and learnt to play the piano and viola. Our home was surrounded with open fields where I spent many hours running about and playing football. Rugby arrived when I went to Tonyrefail Grammar School and came under the influence of Ned Gribble, a magnificent coach and teacher. You see, he believed in talent and style, adventure and hard work. Life, he told us, was exactly like rugby with all the joys and sadness, the elations and disappointments. So very early on in life we learnt to cope with the ups and downs.

Good fortune, and Mr Gribble's influence, made it possible for me to play for Cardiff, the Barbarians and Wales and, in 1955, to be selected for the British and Irish Lions Team to tour South Africa. We were a young team and very few of us had ever travelled abroad or been away from home for any length of time.

The tours in those days lasted four months. The South African experience meant that suddenly all the things we had learnt in geography and history lessons had become a reality. It was, indeed, a wonderful period of my life. The friendships I made with the other members of the team, from all walks of life, the rugby, the people we met in South Africa, the sights we saw. I was so lucky.

# 🫖 Cliff Morgan

When I retired from rugby, good fortune came my way again and an extraordinarily talented broadcaster, Hywel Davies, then Head of Programmes at BBC Wales, asked me to help set up a television sports department. Hywel was the most wonderful mentor and taught me so much. Above all he taught me never, ever to forget that broadcasting was an enormous privilege. He opened the door for me to broadcasting.

That allowed me to enter so many different worlds. With sport I went to Olympic Games, Commonwealth Games, World Cups and World Championships on every continent in the world. As an editor in Current Affairs, I was involved in covering tragic events, such as the Aberfan disaster, politics and the big issues of the day, working with giants of broadcasting like James Cameron, Robert Kee and Alistair Burnett. Then as the Royal Liaison Officer for the BBC, I was closely involved in the programmes covering royal and national Events. Through broadcasting I met so many wonderful people, the bravest and the fittest, the talented and the brightest, the carers and the kindest. What memories!

My life has been so full and rich I find it difficult to name my most pleasurable memories – there are too many of them! I would obviously put at the top of the list the joy my family has given me, the birth of my daughter and son and the pleasure they have given me as they grew up into kind and caring adults with a wonderful zest for life. Now too I have the joy of seeing my grandson grow into manhood with those same delightful qualities and a wiser head on his shoulders than his granddad had at his age!

In rugby one of the highs would have to be the First Test on that Lions Tour in the torrid arena of Ellis Park, Johannesburg. In the heat and altitude of the High Veldt, we were given no chance of winning but it turned out to be full of tough and robust forward play combined with some classy and brilliant running. It was a credit to both teams. The final score was South Africa 22 points, the Lions 23 points!

Of course, like everyone else, I have had my ups and downs. When I was 42, I had a stroke whilst I was in Germany covering a rugby match for the British Forces Broadcasting Service. However, thanks to the good medical care I received, after a year I made an almost full recovery. It was tough, particularly for my wife, as we had a young family and as a freelancer at that time, I was unable to earn any money. However, with the patience and care of family and friends we managed to make it through that difficult time.

Four years ago I had to have my larynx removed when I was diagnosed with cancer of the vocal chords and now I breathe through my neck and speak through a little plastic valve. I have the most brilliant and kind surgeon looking after me and the most caring nurses and, as I had already virtually retired from broadcasting, the loss of my voice hasn't been as bad as it might have been. Besides, I see so many people far worse off than me. Now I live very contentedly on the Isle of Wight with my wife, Pat, in a beautiful part of the island, where the sun always seems to shine and the people all greet you with a big smile. What more could an old man ask for?

## Sylvia Syms

# "I can't see myself ever retiring. What would I do with myself? I think if you asked the majority of actors that same question, they would all give the same answer."

Actress Sylvia Syms hasn't been out of work since she shot to fame in the 1956 box office hit *My Teenage Daughter*. She starred in films such as *Ice-Cold in Alex*, *Victim*, *Conspiracy of Hearts* and *The World of Suzie Wong*, alongside leading men like Orson Welles, John Mills, Anthony Quayle, Roger Moore and Dirk Bogarde. More recently, she was an unforgettable Queen Mother in the film *The Queen*. But work means much more than fame to Sylvia – it's also her way of coping when things go wrong. Sylvia was awarded the OBE in 2007.

Life hasn't always been easy, but thankfully, work has always been there for me.

# Sylvia Syms

I always wanted to be an actress. There was a war on and my father wasn't around very much in my childhood, but when he was there, I remember he took me to the cinema on Saturday mornings, and we went to a lot of shows, concerts and ballet.

When I was just 12, my mother committed suicide. But I remember that she loved books and taught all of us children to read before we went to school.

Two years after her death, my father married Aunt Dorothy, who was a great influence on my life. She encouraged me enormously and was very keen for me to get into drama school. She continued to love all of us children even though my father died young.

Although my career took off, all I really wanted was to have a family. I wanted a home and kids. I wouldn't give up work, but that's what I wanted. I was distraught when my first baby was still-born, and my second, Jessica, lived for only two days. We adopted a baby boy, Ben, and soon afterwards I discovered I was pregnant for the third time with my daughter, Beatie.

I stayed in my marriage far too long – I guess it gave me a feeling of security. I knew it wasn't right. We lived under the same roof but we weren't really living together. But then my husband suddenly confessed that he had been having an affair with a colleague and they had a two-year-old daughter. That was a terrible shock.

Now, I live on my own. I've learnt that it doesn't do to dwell on things, and you have to realise that there are many people who are worse off. I was brought up to feel socially responsible, and that's one of the things about being an actor – ours is a very caring and generous profession. Because we all do a lot of work for charities, we come across people who are really suffering because of poverty, illness or old age.

I can't think of any other profession that does so much to help others. I think it's because luck plays such a big part in our careers. When we achieve some success we are very grateful for everything that comes our way. We want the chance to give something back.

When I was awarded the OBE in 2007, I insisted it should be in recognition of my charity work as well as my career.

I'm lucky that I'm still working – there aren't that many good roles for older women. After making *The Queen* I had a guest spot on *EastEnders* and also had a marvellous time filming *The Poseidon Adventure* in South Africa. It was terribly exciting to do stunts and film underwater.

Work has been my sanctuary, really. I've never earned much money. People think because I'm on the telly and in films I must have pots of it. But after my first film I stupidly signed a contract for £30 a week, which I bitterly regret. I made many of my early films on that 30 quid. I can't see myself ever retiring. What would I do with myself? I think if you asked the majority of actors that same question, they would all give the same answer.

# "The heavy load took its toll on my health. I was working far too hard and taking too much on. Eventually, I suffered a mental breakdown."

**Alex Scott became a beneficiary of Elizabeth Finn Care in 2001. A self professed workaholic, his successful career as a manager of theatre and arts organisations was cut short when he suffered a mental breakdown and then lost his sight to untreatable degenerative glaucoma.**

As a child, my dream was to be a writer. I was very lucky to have been brought up in an academic household where books were cherished, and in which I was encouraged to read a lot and be creative. My mother was an Archaeologist at the British Museum and my father was a solicitor.

I had a flair for creative writing and a storytelling streak. I can still remember my parents' astonishment when, at the age of 14, I came home with a huge electronic typewriter which I hoped would be my tool to further this ambition.

By the time I reached secondary school, I had entertained thoughts of both a legal and then a medical career. The London Underground and London Buses were personal obsessions. Chief Medical Officer for London Transport seemed the ideal job. Eventually, I decided to study Theology at University, and decided perhaps becoming the Archbishop of Canterbury would do!

It was my involvement with student drama which led to the offer of a job as an arts administrator. I soon became a manager of various theatres and arts organisations and my work took me all around the world. It even included training doctors in specialist medicine, setting-up the British Association of Performing Arts Medicine, and advising the Department for International Development. However, the heavy load took its toll on my health. I was working far too hard and taking too much on. Eventually, I suffered a mental breakdown. When I then developed untreatable degenerative glaucoma, my depression became even more severe.

My worsening eyesight, coupled with my state of mind, led me to shut off. I began living a hermit-like existence, losing all pride and self-reliance. I felt so isolated from those around me who were still going on with their lives, dealing with the day-to-day. I didn't want anyone to feel sorry for me or feel I was a burden and I certainly didn't want to ask them for financial help, but the bills were mounting to the point that every day was spent in fear of the bailiffs coming to my door. Eventually they did and I lost practically everything.

It's very difficult to have everything you have worked for in life taken away. Some people say it's freeing to get rid of material possessions and have no financial assets. Maybe it is, until the washing machine breaks down and there is no way you can afford to fix it. Having to go without so-called luxuries is one thing, but when your world falls apart around you, you also have to give up some of your dreams. A lot of the dreams I once had are utterly impossible and unachievable now, and that is perhaps one of the hardest things a person ever has to deal with.

Now, I've re-built my life and formed a new outlook. I can proudly declare myself debt free and, with the help of regular grants from Elizabeth Finn Care, I'm getting along better than ever. I haven't stopped dreaming by any means – I've just had to find new dreams. I'd like to become totally economically self-sufficient and have the opportunity to use my skills and talents. The future is holding out a journey of self-discovery for me and is inviting me to become the person I truly am rather than the person I used to be.

# Lionel Blair

## "We had little in the way of material items, but you didn't necessarily notice things like that back then, as everyone around us was in the same position."

Lionel Blair is one of Britain's most celebrated entertainers, with a career spanning song, dance, choreography, acting and TV presenting. He became a much-loved television favourite as one of the team captains on *Give Us a Clue*, and as the presenter of *Name That Tune*. More recently, he has starred in the West End production of *Chitty Chitty Bang Bang*, hosted the touring show *Simply Ballroom* and is regularly on our screens giving his comments on the stars of *Strictly Come Dancing* in the spin-off show, *It Takes Two*.

I grew up in Tottenham in the 1940s and I suppose, looking back, we were poor really. We had little in the way of material items, but you didn't necessarily notice things like that back

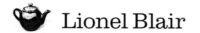 

then, as everyone around us was in the same position. We were all proud, working class families: my mother stayed at home while my father worked as a barber. We never went without food or clothing, but there was little in the way of luxuries.

From an early age, I was fascinated with performing and my parents really supported me and my sister Joyce in our love of the stage. I acquired my first pair of tap shoes at the age of six – I can't remember exactly how much they cost, but I know it would have been more than they could afford at the time. It never really occurred to me until later in life that performing might have been a strange profession to encourage a boy to go into – my father must have been very open-minded and didn't mind a jot that his son was more into singing and dancing than playing sport.

Sadly my father passed away when I was 15, which meant that I became the head of the family. At the time I was in a musical in the West End called *Bob's Your Uncle* and earning £10 a week. I then went straight off to Scotland for a summer season at the Ayr Gaiety Theatre.

Although I'd got used to making a living as a performer by then, the fact that I was now the main breadwinner was a pretty big responsibility for a boy of that age, but it gave me even more motivation to get more work and earn more money to take home to my family.

They say 'There's no business like show business' and it really is true. I've had a wonderful life and have met so many inspiring people along the way. I've gone from performing in London Underground stations during the Blitz to dancing in front of royalty at the Palladium with my late, great, best friend, Sammy Davis Junior.

Perhaps one of my proudest achievements is the fact that I've been able to help so many young dancers and performers throughout my career. A young Elaine Paige got a break as part of the chorus for a show I did with BBC TV called *68 Style*. Funnily enough, a young man who I believe became pretty well known also auditioned, but I turned him down. At that time, Ziggy Stardust was probably just a twinkle in his eye, but David Bowie did, in fact, audition for my chorus line. I suppose he would have been about 20. I felt he was just too different, too eye catching to be a member of the ensemble. To me, he was a standout performer. Turns out, I was right!

# Seeta Indrani

# "There were times when I'd feel a little under the weather but would still go on and try to sing through it."

Known to millions as WPC Norika Datta in *The Bill*, for which she won Best Actress and Best Supporting Actress (Asian Film Academy), Seeta made her stage debut as Cassandra in the original production of Andrew Lloyd-Webber's *CATS*. She has also worked with The Royal Shakespeare Company, Royal National Theatre and Rambert Dance Company. She appeared at the London Palladium with childhood heroine Cyd Charisse and took part in the first national tour for 40 years of Britain's oldest opera company, Carl Rosa Opera Company, playing Prince Orlovsky in *Die Fledermaus*. She is currently appearing as Dr Lily Hassan in the BBC series, *Doctors*.

In 2001, I did a three-month tour of Australia and New Zealand in Gilbert and Sullivan's *The Mikado*, in which I played the role of Pitti Sing.

The tour covered a huge area. We flew into Melbourne and from there we traveled to Sydney, Newcastle and Perth. After we finished the shows in Australia, we went on to New Zealand, where we did performances in Auckland and Christchurch.

# Seeta Indrani

I found the tour arduous, not only because of its length and the fact that it was on the other side of the world, but because of the amount of publicity that we did for the show. It was pretty constant throughout the three months: I did live radio interviews, interviews with magazines and newspapers as well as TV appearances. It could be quite manic. I would be in the car on the way to a radio station, while recording a telephone interview with another station as we drove – that's how busy we were!

I arrived in Melbourne a week before the rest of the company to do interviews and publicity. There was no time to get over jet lag. Within 24 hours of arriving, I was doing my first radio slot, with a full day of publicity – starting with an appearance on Good Morning Australia – scheduled for the next day. I remember I was quite jet lagged and not quite with it, so I accidentally called the radio presenter by the wrong name! By the time we got to New Zealand, I was exhausted.

Whenever I am offered a singing role – especially in opera – I always accept the job with a certain degree of trepidation. Opera singers have to be very careful with their voices; they make sure that they protect them and rest them when needed, so that they remain strong. You spend your life trying to avoid losing your voice: you become sensitive to dust and dryness, you have to be careful of people with colds and if you go to a bar with loud music, you have to take care not to shout over the top of it so that you don't damage your voice.

Because *The Bill* has a strong following in Australia and New Zealand, I felt an obligation to be on stage for every performance. I didn't want to let anybody down. So there were times when I'd feel a little under the weather but would still go on and try to sing through it. Only once was I so ill, that I couldn't go on – I'd dragged myself down to the theatre, only to be met with: "What are you doing here?" and was promptly sent straight back home to bed.

When you're on a tour that has a heavy schedule, you have to shut down your life. I always liken myself to an athlete who's in training; I have to be that disciplined. I have to take care of my health because I can't afford to get ill and affect the performance. Whenever I'm doing operas, I basically live like a nun. I don't drink alcohol, I eat really well and I make sure I get lots of sleep. That's the only way to get through it.

# Diana Moran

# "I was diagnosed with breast cancer at the age of 47. I was terrified."

Diana Moran, TV's Green Goddess, was the famous face of fitness on *BBC Breakfast* when it began 26 years ago. She is now an author, broadcaster, presenter and cruise ship lecturer.

I was diagnosed with breast cancer at the age of 47. I was terrified. I was the BBC's Green Goddess, the nation's gym mistress. I felt desperately alone. John and I had separated a year before. I was on the crest of a wave with my campaign on *BBC Breakfast: Get Britain Fit*. Cancer happens to other people, we all know that. My thought at that moment was, "I don't want my life to stop. I've got so much more I want to do". And the biggest thing at that moment was, "I want to see my boys with partners and I want to see some grandchildren."

I decided to keep it a secret. I told a close friend and my agent. They made me tell my two sons, and the boys told John. So now there were just six of us who knew. Eventually, after two weeks of deliberating, I went back to see the surgeons to say I wasn't going to have anything done but by the time I came out I had conceded to their recommendations of a bilateral mastectomy followed by immediate reconstruction, about which I knew zilch.

# 🫖 Diana Moran

I was booked into the hospital under my maiden name. The operation was a very big shock. I felt mutilated. I was proud of my body but, more than that, it was part of the tools of my trade. I had high levels of fitness and that got me over the operation, but mentally I was in a mess. I couldn't talk to people. I now know you must talk to people, which is why I encourage people to discuss their problems.

I was spiritual; I talked to my God quite a lot, and eventually I found the best way to cope with my problem was to write it all down. So every day I wrote down what was happening to me physically, but also spiritually and mentally. I was coping because of an inner strength brought out in me as a small child by my disciplined and disciplining father, who taught me to stand on my own two feet.

Harold Evans, then Editor of *The Sunday Times*, heard from a friend that I had been keeping a very detailed diary. He said it would be important to share it with other cancer patients and that's how I came to publish the book, which I called *A More Difficult Exercise* – the diary of six months of my life.

It was launched in the lecture theatre of the Royal Marsden Hospital, because the surgeons were thrilled that somebody was finally coming out so positively about having cancer. But some of the press coverage was hurtful. A male journalist in *The Mirror* wrote: "Green Goddess has breast cancer. If that's what keeping fit does for you, I'll stick to walking my dog."

Immediately it was out in the open, I started my work with cancer charities. I am celebrity ambassador for Breast Cancer

Care, for Breakthrough Cancer, patron of the Breast Cancer Campaign and of the Cancer Counselling Trust. And there are many more.

I now know that the support you get from other women who've been on this journey is vital. Before we start the Breast Cancer Care Ribbon Walks, I do a mass workout; thousands of women in front of me, bending and shaking to my command! We have four this year. We all support one another because we've all gone through the experience of breast cancer – usually ourselves but also in memory, or thanks, for somebody close to us.

I relax by painting, whenever possible out in the fresh air. I sit by the river and capture light. I've painted on and off during my life, probably when I've had my most down moments. That's when I resort to the paint. It has to be oil, it has to be thick; it can be put on with a knife as well as brushes; it's not delicate stuff, it's strong stuff, and it's absolutely passionate. When I paint I don't eat, I don't see anything or anybody; I'm absolutely in a world of my own and I'm never happier.

## Canon Roger Royle

# "They were afraid where no fear was."

**Canon Roger Royle is a clergyman, broadcaster, writer and occasional pantomime dame. He presented *Sunday Half Hour* on Radio 2 for 16 years until his retirement in 2007. He is a regular contributor to *Pause for Thought* on *Wake Up to Wogan* and can also be heard from time to time presenting *Good Morning Sunday*.**

I describe myself as an "allsorts" with maverick tendencies. I am the son of a clergyman, but sadly my father died when I was one. Not having a father from the word go had an enormous effect. It was ages before I could spell the word "father" – I spelt it "farther". I didn't know how to cope with friends' fathers, because I wasn't used to having one around the house.

The loss stayed with me, but my mother was such a powerful person to me, so important and always has been. I was 18 when she died. I always steadfastly keep her anniversary – with rejoicing, with happiness, with fun; and yes, with tears, but it's not a mournful day by any means. I think my parents were responsible for the two prime influences in my life – the Church and the theatre.

I do have a problem in that I'm not brilliant at commitment. Maybe it's a result of losing parents at an early age, and a feeling of not wanting to be let down again.

# Canon Roger Royle

When I was a child, my mother and I went to the pantomime at the New Theatre, Cardiff. I always tried to be the first to go up on stage, embarrassing my brother Peter terribly. I went to the twice-nightly variety shows in Cardiff and when I was older I took my mother to the cinema.

I loved the ritual of church, the splendid costumes – the vestments; it was very theatrical. So I went straight from school to read Theology at Kings College, London. I was ordained in the Church of England in 1962 and became a curate, one of 11, at St Mary's in Portsmouth. That was a brilliant experience, a marvellous training parish, and I still have friends there.

From Portsmouth I went to the St Helier housing estate and hospital in south London. For the first six months I didn't fit in at all: they didn't get my sense of humour and I didn't get theirs. The parish pantomime was my salvation. Drama came to the rescue.

One of the biggest eye-openers in my life was when I went to be chaplain of Lord Mayor Treloar School & College for people with physical disabilities.

The world of disability had a profound effect on me. I saw how parents and siblings coped with disability within the family and the colossal stress on all involved.

Coping with bereavement has always been very, very important to me. Having suffered it myself I never wanted people to think they weren't cared for at times like that. I introduced a Thanksgiving Assembly for students who had died. It meant tears, but that's part of grieving. And, if the parents agreed, students who were mates could go to the funeral. Then back to College for tea, a celebratory wake. It did make a difference.

I feel the pressure of caring for people, particularly after a suicide. Worrying whether you're getting it right, balancing things properly. Preparation is hugely important and I get up very early in the morning. I need to check things through, sort things out. I can give the appearance of spur of the moment but it's been very well planned and packaged.

If I'm out of sorts with friends, it really drags me down. In adversity I need God and friends in equal parts. At times I have been afraid of things when I shouldn't have been. I think many of us are afraid of things when we shouldn't be. We turn them into huge problems when there's no reason to be fearful. I take comfort from the old prayer book version of Psalm 53: "They were afraid where no fear was."

## Rakie Ayola

# "I took her on a trip with my husband and oldest daughter. I surprised her by letting her watch a scan of her fourth granddaughter. She'd never seen a scan before. She burst into tears."

**Actress Rakie Ayola carved out a highly successful theatre and radio career before becoming a well-known face on our screens, starring in several TV dramas including *Doctor Who*, *Soldier, Soldier*, *Sea Of Souls* and three series of the BBC medical drama, *Holby City as* Nurse Kyla Tyson. She has also appeared in Hollywood films *The I Inside* and *Sahara*.**

Effectively, I've had two sets of parents in my life, but I've only met my real mother three times and I never met my real father. My birth mother left me when I was a few weeks old to travel around the world studying and I was brought up by

her cousin and his wife in Cardiff. They were always very open about the fact that they weren't my "real" parents but they were amazing. They never criticised my mother or made me feel that I was a burden to them.

It took me a long time to acknowledge the anger I felt towards my birth mother, which I think was exacerbated by the death of my adoptive mum when I was 14. She was everything to me and when she finally succumbed to cancer I was devastated.

While expecting my second child I realised that I had to confront the negative feelings that have informed so much of my life. I decided to set up a meeting with my mother while she was visiting from Sierra Leone.

At first, sitting across a table from her felt awkward, but after the initial polite small talk, we began to really talk to each other. At one point she asked me what I thought of her and I saw that as my cue to be completely honest. I'm sure it wasn't as painful for me to say as it was for her to hear. There were tears when I finally told her that I forgive her. It sounded pompus when said out loud but I was relieved to be able to say it and mean it. That meeting ended with us hugging and me calling her mum for the first time.

It seemed appropriate to mark our "new" relationship somehow, so a few days later I took her on a trip with my husband and oldest daughter. I surprised her by letting her watch a scan of her fourth granddaughter. She'd never seen a scan before. She burst into tears.

As a child, it's impossible to understand how someone can leave you to make your own way in the world. I was angry, hurt and confused by my mum's decision. I think that becoming a mother myself gave me perspective and I can see now that she did what was right for her at the time. Besides, my Cardiff upbringing has made me the person and the mother I am, so how can I regret or want to change that?

🫖 David Moore

# "The authorities slapped a dangerous buildings order on us and the five storey town house had to be torn down."

**David Moore began his career at Raymond Blanc's Manoir Aux Quatre Saisons in Oxford and, within three years, became assistant manager. In 1991, he opened the restaurant Pied à Terre and has since gone on to open L'Autre Pied and a further restaurant in Harrogate. Most recently, he has been on our screens as one of the Inspectors in the BBC 2 series *The Restaurant*.**

It was 8.30am and I was in France at a wine tasting when I got the phone call saying that Charlotte Street was cordoned off and there were three fire engines outside our restaurant, Pied à Terre. I got back to find that the whole place was totally destroyed. The authorities slapped a dangerous buildings order on us and the five storey town house had to be torn down. 14 years of work and two Michelin stars had effectively gone up in smoke.

It was a complete change of life. Up until that moment, I had lived and breathed the day-to-day of running a restaurant.

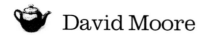 David Moore

My first job straight out of Catering College was waiting on at Raymond Blanc's Manoir Aux Quatre Saisons.

After three years I had worked my way up the ranks to become Assistant Manager and stayed on in that role for another three years before taking the plunge of opening 'Pied àTerre' at the age of 26. Within four years, we had two Michelin stars.

Although it put us out of business for a year, the fire was actually fortuitous. It gave me perspective and more time to look at life, how I was spending my time and what I still wanted to achieve.

I couldn't have opened my own restaurant in the first place without the financial backing of several influential and high profile customers I'd met at Le Manoir. Plus, Raymond had totally embraced the idea, giving us his full backing.

Having been lucky enough to have him help us up the ladder, I realised that I wanted to do the same. The time away from the daily routine allowed me, together with our former sous chef, Marcus Eaves, to open our sister restaurant, L'Autre Pied.

Last year it was awarded its first Michelin star. I've also been involved with a venture up in Harrogate, helping another young chef realise his dream of opening his own restaurant.

Nowadays I've taken a step back and, although I love being at the restaurant, I know that our manager can actually run it much better on a day-to-day basis than I can. More free time has also allowed me a little TV career on the side too, which I've loved. I've been recognised by a few cabbies, but I certainly don't think of myself as some famous celebrity. At the end of the day, I'm a lucky waiter really – I was in the right place at the right time.

## Amanda Waring

# "I think if you have such a difficult illness to fight, your spirits need to be strong."

**Amanda Waring is an actress, director and producer and daughter of acclaimed actress Dame Dorothy Tutin. She starred as *Gigi* in the acclaimed West End Musical and sang at the Royal Variety Show for the Queen. Amanda's one woman show *For the Love of Chocolate* premiered at the Edinburgh Festival and has been critically acclaimed wherever it's been performed.**

When Mama was in hospital with leukaemia, I was outraged by the lack of compassion she received – and the impact this had on her mind, body and spirit.

Doctors and nurses treated her as if she was invisible. There was no eye contact, no sense of dignity or respect. I don't think they were being deliberately cruel but there was no understanding that emotional care is as important as good medical practice. It only takes a second to look someone in the eye, touch them on the hand or call them by the right name. They're small things but they make a huge difference.

Mama said she felt like a caged animal and I saw how she started to withdraw and decline.

We moved her to another hospital. It was a big step but I know we made the right decision. Staff there saw Mama as an individual rather than part of a category. They were friendly and communicative and Mama's spirits and health improved immediately. I think if you have such a difficult illness to fight, your spirits need to be strong. But that can be taken away in a heartbeat by thoughtless and insensitive behaviour.

During the last 18 months of her life, Mama managed so

many important milestones – she received her Damehood at Buckingham Palace, attended my brother's wedding and saw the birth of my son Ben. She spent her final days at a MacMillan hospital with wonderful nurses who really understood the importance of seeing – and treating – the whole person.

When Mama died I was determined to highlight the need for a change in attitudes towards older people and the importance of dignity and respect for patients of all ages. I sold my flat to make a film called *What Do You See*. Virginia McKenna, a special friend, stars in the film, playing an older woman being cared for in hospital. She speaks the moving words of a poem written by Phyllis McCormack, a nurse who worked with elderly patients:

*But inside this old carcass a young girl still dwells,*
*and now and again my battered heart swells.*
*I remember the joys, I remember the pain,*
*and I'm loving and living life over again.*

*I think of the years; all too few, gone too fast,*
*and accept the stark fact that nothing can last.*
*So open your eyes, nurses, open and see,*
*not a crabbit old woman; look closer - see ME!!*

It's a powerful film that has been shown all around the world, raising awareness of the need to respect older people, and raising money for charity as well.

I've just finished my second film, also starring Virginia, which examines the emotional journey that older people make when they enter residential care.

I'm also working on a film about our attitudes to death and end of life care. I feel very strongly that we should be able to walk hand in hand with death as many other cultures do, and release some of the fear surrounding it.

As a result of the films, I've been asked to talk at conferences around the world and wanted to get those ideas into a training pack. I worked with care expert Rosemary Hurtley to devise a resource to really bring home the concept of dignity in care. It is for nurses, doctors, care workers – across the board – with fun exercises as well as serious messages about our attitudes to ageing.

As an actress I have been paralysed with nerves on occasion and I'm sometimes surprised that I can stand up in front of audiences and talk about the way we care for older people. But when your subject matter is bigger than you are, hopefully your ego isn't in the way. Great satisfaction comes from knowing you are making a difference.

## Jeffrey Holland

# "He dressed me down for being unprofessional and said I should have stayed."

Jeffrey had no real aspirations to act until a friend suggested they go to local drama group for something to do. He has since appeared in roles from Shakespeare and drama to comedy, musicals and pantomime. In 1975, Jeffrey joined the cast of the musical stage version of *Dad's Army* in which he took over the role of Cockney spiv Private Walker. His TV debut came in *Dixon of Dock Green* and was quickly followed by roles in *Are You Being Served*, *It Ain't Half Hot Mum* and *Hi de Hi*.

In 1976, my first wife was pregnant. Her obstetric history wasn't good; this was her fourth pregnancy so, naturally, we were very worried.

I was in Richmond, playing Private Walker in *Dad's Army*. My wife was at home in Coventry where we lived and had gone for a routine antenatal check-up. She was not due for another week or two, so was surprised when the doctor announced that she was in labour. She was having contractions she didn't even know about!

# 🫖 Jeffrey Holland

When I got the news just before the finale of the matinee, I flew into a complete panic. I needed to be there with her – she was in danger. I did the finale, we took the curtain call and I was off. I told the boys who were covering for me: "Lads, you're on tonight – wife's having a baby. I'm off. Bye!" That was it.

Of course, my actions were unprofessional; in acting, the show must go on regardless. But to me, my wife's life was much more important than a play. And it was only a play after all, it wasn't real life – but she was.

I legged it as fast as I could. I just leapt on the first train I could find and when I arrived in Coventry, jumped the taxi queue. I said: "Excuse me, wife's having a baby – got to go!" and I was there. It took me less than three hours.

Fortunately I was in time. She was in chronic labour for hours and hours and didn't have the baby until half past two. Then, a bouncing baby boy was born, a big lad: ten pounds two and a quarter ounces. But there were complications; they had to keep her in hospital and look after her.

The next day, I went back to the theatre wondering what kind of reaction I was in for – especially from the stars of the show. I was summoned to Arthur Lowe's dressing room as soon as I got in. I was nervous as I knocked on his door and he bellowed out: "Come in!" He really told me off. He dressed me down for being unprofessional and said I should have stayed and done the show. The show was more important, he said, babies were born all the time.

I was so determined to put him in the picture that I told him exactly what was going on and why I had left the show so dramatically. He sort of "harrumphed" and we carried on and finished the show with no further incidents.

But the lovely thing was that the first flowers to arrive at my wife's bedside were from the Lowes.

## Judy Buxton

# "I was still broken-hearted about losing James and I just wanted to get away."

**Judy has had huge successes in repertory theatre, in the West End and with the Royal Shakespeare Company. Her many and varied TV appearances include roles in *Lovejoy*, *Bergerac*, *Rising Damp*, *Next of Kin* and three series of *On The Up* opposite Dennis Waterman. Film credits include *Aces High*, *The Likely Lads*, *The Big Sleep* and *Get Real*.**

I was with my partner, James, for many years. We never married but lived together for a very long time. Sadly, in 1994, James was diagnosed with cancer. It was a very sudden thing and he passed away in November of that year. I was devastated.

I'd already met Jeffrey when we were in a play together at Windsor Theatre. This was before James became ill and Jeffrey was married at the time. There was nothing in it: I just remember thinking that Jeffrey was a great actor and a very nice person.

About a year after James died, Derek Nimmo – an actor who is sadly no longer with us – offered me a job. It was a comedy that I had done before called *Out of Order* by Ray Cooney. Derek would organise these dinner theatre tours to take people across to the Far East and Middle East, and this was

one of those tours. I jumped at the chance; I was still broken-hearted about losing James and I just wanted to get away.

Funnily enough, Derek's son had phoned me to ask whether I knew of a suitable actor to play the character of George Picton. Off-hand, I couldn't think of anyone but told him I would have a think about it.

Then, one evening, I was sitting at home and suddenly thought: "Gosh, Jeffrey Holland would have been good at that character – he'd have been brilliant!" It was too late by then to mention it so imagine my surprise when we started rehearsals to find that Jeffrey had been cast in the role!

So we went off on tour to the Far East and Middle East. Jeffrey had obviously heard about James, but what I didn't realise at the time was that Jeffrey's marriage was in trouble. I was still very vulnerable because of what had happened to me. In hindsight, it was almost as if fate intervened so that we were cast in these roles and that we were able to provide each other with a shoulder to cry on.

We were able to support each other and Jeffrey's companionship helped ease the heartbreak of losing James. We were both grieving the loss of our relationships and understood what each other was going through.

Over time, our friendship grew into love and we are now happily married. I consider myself truly lucky to be given this second chance at love!

Tea & Teardrops

 Bill Tidy

# "It was the unfairness of it that got to me – that anyone should outlive their children."

**Bill Tidy is a cartoonist, writer and television personality acclaimed for his comic strips *The Cloggies* in Private Eye and *The Fosdyke Saga* in The Mirror. He is known for his charitable work, particularly for The Lord's Taverners. He was awarded the MBE in 2000.**

I lost my son, Nick, a couple of years ago, when he was 38 years old. That changes your attitude and makes you more caring and close to those of your family who are still with you. Not that there was any division between us, but it makes you doubly appreciative. My wife Rosa really cracked up. I think women mourn in a completely different way to men. I don't know – you just plod on. It helps if you're busy. You can do jobs to forget.

It was the unfairness of it that got to me – that anyone should outlive their children. That's so appalling, yet when it happens to you, you're astonished at the number of people who contact you who have suffered the same thing. Rosa helped me, and I helped her. Someone you've been with for a long time and thinks the same way that you do is an enormous support. We've been married for 49 years. Next

# Bill Tidy

year's the big one!

Sylvia, my daughter, is another driving force in my life. She's my agent and still thinks I'm 25, which is nice. She's even got me on to Twitter.

I have always drawn. I remember as a child drawing on the tops of the waxed paper that used to be on jars of jam. I'd be about four, and I would go to the shop with my mother and she'd say, "Look what he can do!" I'd draw a cowboy and we may have got the jam at a reduced price.

I never even met another cartoonist until I'd been going a year or two, and then the Cartoonist Club of Great Britain was formed. I palled up with Larry, a great cartoonist from Birmingham, because we were provincials. In those days it was desperate to be provincials. I'm a Scouser – Anfield. I lived about 40 yards from the ground and walked across the park to see the Blues.

As a cartoonist it's not necessarily about grabbing the first idea that comes along. You have to say to yourself: Well, if that's the first that's come into my head, it must be the first that's come into everybody's, so just see if there's another hidden flower in that clump. And the guys who I respect also do that.

It was a tremendous time for me when *The Fosdyke Saga* got into The Mirror and *The Cloggies* in Private Eye. They each ran for about 15 years. For those two to come along and give me a regular income was absolutely fabulous.

I've been on the fringes of showbusiness, the entertainment world for years, but I'm no threat to anyone. I'm not a comic, an actor or a presenter so I'm not stealing their material. People often think you're dead if you don't do television, but I seem to get rediscovered about once every four years.

I support The Lord's Taverners 100 per cent, but there's something about Elizabeth Finn Care that I find fascinating. It began by helping 'distressed gentlefolk' – that was a term of its day. It means the same today – helping decent people. I don't know how it will cope with what's going to happen over the next year or so. The charity's going to be flooded with requests for help and I wish it all the luck in the world. There will be more people whose lives have been proceeding on a proper course who suddenly hit the rocks. It could be me, it could be anyone.

## Sarah-Jane Honeywell

# "I kept my condition a secret – nobody knew about it."

**Sarah-Jane Honeywell has worked in the entertainment industry for many years. Famous for her work as a comedy actress, with over 30 episodes of *Higgledy House* currently showing across the world, she is also well-known as a children's TV presenter with the BBC's magazine show *Tikkabilla*.**

Like most people who are affected by bulimia, I kept my condition a secret – nobody knew about it.

I began my career as a dancer. Because I am only 4 foot 11, there was enormous pressure on me to be thin. I remember when I was just starting out, someone told me: "Your boobs are too big, you'll never be a dancer". This remark stuck with me throughout my struggle with bulimia. Even when I proved to myself that I could be a dancer by getting into *Cats* from an open audition, it was still there in my head: I was too big.

I was 19 when I moved to London to do *Cats*. I lived on my own and kept to myself; I was very quiet and shy, so it was easy to keep my bulimia a secret. After *Cats* I found an acting job. So, on paper, I looked like a very successful girl: I had bought a little flat of my own and I was doing well in my

career. In reality, it was quite a different story. I was totally out of control. I felt I had no power over who I was; bulimia had that control.

When I was 22 years old, I met a guy. He was very abusive. Bulimia makes you lose touch with your emotions, you become numb. In that state, it's easy to let people abuse you because you are completely unaware of yourself. It's almost as if it has a magic spell on you.

Even though the guy was violent, I thought I could fix him. Even though I should have been helping myself, I wanted to help him. Sometimes I think that's why you stay with men like that – not because you're a victim, but because you think you can help them.

So, at the time, I was dealing with my bulimia – this all-consuming, terrible secret – and also having to deal with this horrible man. I was feeling more and more helpless and spiralling further and further out of control. It was getting to the point where I felt that if something didn't happen to help me, I couldn't face going on.

All the stress, all the hurt, all the anguish and all the fear culminated one day when I completely lost it: I was in a local supermarket and I suddenly started smashing up an Easter Egg display. Although it was very dramatic – and perhaps a little crazy – it was the best thing that ever happened to me because it meant I had to confront the unhealthy aspects of my life at last. I had to confront my bulimia and I had to confront the guy. I had to stand up and say: "Not only are you ruining yourself with food, you're putting up with these things that you really shouldn't."

I was very lucky; I went to an Eating Disorder Clinic and I eventually got rid of the guy. While the clinic helped me I realised I really didn't know how to eat, that I was afraid of food. What helped me through this dark period was a book that is now out of print, a book by Dr Cherie Martin called, *Naturally Slim Without Dieting*. It taught me that I could eat what I wanted if I just listened to my own body. Since then, I have adhered to the book's guidelines and have maintained the same weight since.

I no longer have bulimia and have been living with my partner – an amazing man – for more than 10 years. He makes me so happy. So even though it sounds horrible – smashing up an Easter Egg display – it really wasn't that bad. I believe it was just what I needed to wake me up.

## Francoise Pascal

# "I learnt a great lesson from this trip, that whenever you feel like giving up, there is always someone around to help you and keep you going through the tough times."

Francoise Pascal made her name with Peter Sellers in the 1970 film *There's a Girl in My Soup.* Her credits vary from *Terry and June* to Hollywood drama *The Young and The Restless,* but Francoise is perhaps best known for playing saucy Danielle Favre in 70s sitcom, *Mind Your Language.*

When I was asked to join a trekking trip to Egypt for a charity I jumped at the opportunity to raise funds for such a worthwhile cause. But underneath my excitement I was very nervous: the thought of walking 112 miles in the space of five days felt like a huge challenge, especially as I was in my fifties. I quickly set to work on building up my strength and endurance.

# Francoise Pascal

I spent months following a gruelling fitness plan and stuck to a healthy diet – I lost four stone in that period. After lots of hard work, the big day finally dawned and before I knew it I was in Egypt climbing steep terrain and trudging through sand.

The first morning we got up at 5am to climb up a mountain and I was ready for action. The change in climate, however, made for tough walking conditions and half way up, my legs turned to jelly and my feet started slipping about on the slope. All the training I had done disappeared out the window at this point and other members of the group had to push me up the slope. At the time I was really mad with myself but I smile now when I recall this memory.

Day one done and still a 112-mile trek to get through. At that point I did question whether I could get through the rest of the trip, but with the charity in mind I knew I had to continue.

The following day we set off on our long journey through the desert. The rest of the group were in their 20s and 30s so they were much fitter than myself, but one of them always stayed with me to keep my morale up.

At times I often felt like giving up; blisters and pain wearing me down. But the others kept me going, especially my friend Peter who crossed the 'imaginary' finishing line with me five days later – we still keep in touch today. I learnt a great lesson from this trip, that whenever you feel like giving up, there is always someone around to help you and keep you going through the tough times.

But it wasn't just the endurance side of the trek where I needed a helping hand from my new found family. I couldn't put a tent up to save my life – it kept blowing away, so everyone else would have to help me peg mine up. It came as no surprise when at the end of the trip I won the award for 'worst person to put up a tent'.

There was also the time when I clumsily erased all my pictures on my camera close to the end of the trip. I could have kicked myself, but everyone came to the rescue and sent me all their photographs. This is what friendship is all about – helping people out wherever you can. Even small, thoughtful gestures like this mean the world to the people on the receiving end.

# Simon Weston

## "I had lost so much weight, they had to rebuild me physically."

**In 1982 the RFA Sir Galahad was destroyed in Bluff Cove off the Falkland Islands. On board was Welsh Guardsman Simon Weston – a name and face that became famous for his struggle to overcome his injuries and redefine his role in life. Simon was awarded the OBE in 1992.**

It's funny what they say about a cup of tea helping you through hard times because having a cup of tea with the nurses at the Queen Elizabeth Military Hospital was the first thing my mother used to do before coming in to visit me. A district nurse herself, she needed that cuppa to steel herself for the ordeal of seeing her son.

In those early months of my recovery – receiving the best treatment from a hugely dedicated group of doctors and nurses – I was in a very fragile condition. I had 46 per cent burns and it was touch and go whether I would survive. Half my body was scarred and burnt and I had lost a huge amount of weight. Here was a former seventeen-and-a-half stone rugby prop forward in the Welsh Guards down to eight stone. It was very distressing for Mam and the rest of the family.

Mam, my late step-father and my grandparents, used to make the 500-mile round trip from south Wales up to the hospital in London every week to see me. It must have been

exhausting for them, particularly during the first year of my recovery when I was undergoing so many operations.

My mother literally wanted to give her skin to me so I could get better. It wasn't possible of course but that tells you everything about her as a person. I was fortunate enough to have been brought up surrounded by love and you realise that when parents love, they love unconditionally.

As well as having such superb medical treatment and care, I managed to get through that time by a combination of three things: firstly, the love and support of my family and friends, secondly, the camaraderie and banter with my fellow patients and hospital staff and … lots of eggs.

That last part needs explaining. Because I had lost so much weight, they had to rebuild me physically – so they put me on a huge calorie-intake diet. Thousands of calories were poured into me every day, mainly in the form of eggs and copious amounts of coca cola. It took time, but the eggs and cola diet worked.

It may seem strange considering the seriousness of the injuries, but we had some great laughs at the hospital. Us being military types, a lot of it was black humour. Things that others would wince at would be funny to us. But I won't relate the incident about the nurse and the lad with the embarrassing skin graft!

There was some larking around too. Once when I was coming round from 14 hours of surgery, some of the boys were playing football in the corridor and accidentally smashed a glass partition. A nurse came up to my bed clutching the ball and demanded mock-seriously: "Did you do this?" Despite being on drips and medication, I just had to laugh.

I'm still in touch with my friends from the Welsh Guards. We went through a lot together, good times and bad, and friendships like that are for life. My mates from south Wales were a great support too. They'd be out on the town on a Saturday night and then get into a transit van to come up to London to see me on the Sunday – some of them still going strong from the night before!

I couldn't see a future for myself when I got injured. I certainly never envisaged that I would become a so-called public figure. I don't sing, I don't dance, I don't play football and I'm not good looking.

But I realised that I wanted to do something with my brain. I'd been used to a macho lifestyle which was rough and tough and brutal in some ways. I wanted to prove to myself that I had a brain and could use it.

A few years later, I met Lucy, now my wife and mother of our three children, and everything changed again. Her fantastic support is yet another example of how fortunate I have been with the people in my life.

# Judith Chalmers

# "Family was always so important in my childhood."

Judith Chalmers is well-known as a broadcaster but describes herself primarily as a 'wife, mother and grandmother'. Her family has always been her mainstay – and a source of huge support and encouragement. Judith was awarded the OBE in 1994.

I was at school in Manchester when an elocution teacher suggested my mother write to the Children's Department of the BBC in Manchester asking if I could have an audition. I started by acting in plays and at 17 I was introducing a teenage magazine programme. Trevor Hill was Head of Afternoon & Children's Programmes and he started *Television Club* on which I worked, and which was a forerunner of *Blue Peter*.

My second, and last, audition was to be a BBC television announcer in London. No one in the South could believe they were auditioning a girl from the North of England. I passed and spent nine great years as a senior announcer for BBC television, presenting *Come Dancing*, doing fashion commentaries from Ascot and Henley, and reporting for television news.

In the 70s I was offered my own afternoon programme by Thames Television and we covered every subject under the

sun. We believed we could make a difference. There was one programme on incontinence in women which drew 30,000 responses. As a result of presenting the programme, the Women's National Cancer Control Campaign asked me to do an appeal on television to raise funds to get mobile clinics for cervical smear tests. In those days we needed to take the clinics to where the women were. As a result of the appeal we raised money for two vehicles which parked in shopping centres and supermarket car parks. The WNCCC was reaching out to women – now thankfully those tests are part of mainstream NHS testing.

In 1973, ITV decided to start a holiday programme – *Wish You Were Here...?* – and thought I would be suitable as its presenter as it was women who were doing most of family holiday bookings. I was very fortunate to have that job, which took me around the world.

I have to thank my husband, Neil Durden-Smith, that I was able to balance travelling and the family. We've been married 45 years now and we met when he was a BBC producer after leaving the Royal Navy. When he finished broadcasting – his commentating included *Test Match Special*, the Olympic Games and Trooping the Colour – his public relations and sports sponsorship companies were based in London so he was usually at home, giving tremendous support to our children, Emma and Mark. The family comes first.

Family was always so important in my childhood. It was my mother, Millie, of course who started me off on this interesting career. She was widowed at 44 – my father was only 48 –

but she carried on. She went back to work as secretary to the Matron at the Christie Hospital in Manchester, and made sure my sister's and my education was fully there, encouraging us all the way.

In September 1993, the family had a great party in Portugal to celebrate Neil's birthday. We had only just got back to the UK when mummy had a stroke.

My sister and I drove straight up to Macclesfield Hospital in Cheshire. Our articulate, strong mother could not speak. Over the next two days she gradually began to recover, eventually saying our names. Our family, who had always relied on talking over everything together, began to communicate again.

She asked me about a book I had been writing which was due to be launched in London. I said it would go ahead without me. She said that was nonsense; I must be there and what was I going to wear? I agreed to take the early train from Macclesfield. She made me promise to make sure I had my lipstick on!

Four hours after I left she had another stroke and died in my sister's arms. She had been our guide and mentor, the most precious of mothers. Without her, our lives would have been so much the poorer.

Neil said to me, as he does when things are difficult, or sad: "Just crack on. After all, Millie would have expected nothing less of you."

### Clare Winsor

# "When I finally escaped, I left with absolutely nothing."

**Clare Winsor had just escaped from an abusive marriage when she approached Elizabeth Finn Care for help. She was forced to run away from her home with two of her three children, with little money and no possessions to her name. A beneficiary for five years, Clare no longer receives financial support from Elizabeth Finn Care, but works to raise awareness of the charity, and other organisations that can help people through times of emotional and financial difficulty.**

I was really on my knees when I first approached Elizabeth Finn Care for help. I had to get out of my marriage, as the abuse I had suffered for years became intolerable. As my children were growing up, I also became more and more concerned about the effect the abuse was having on them.

When I finally escaped, I left with absolutely nothing but a huge sense of relief and elation. At the same time, my heart was also breaking, as I was forced to leave my youngest child behind. It has taken a heartbreaking eight years to get him back into my life on a regular basis.

My children and I were placed in a bed and breakfast and then temporary accommodation for four months until we

were found a house to call our own. I wasn't working and just having enough money to keep my car going was a struggle. A close friend of mine, who had also been helped by Elizabeth Finn Care, recommended I call them to see if I qualified for assistance. I was amazed at the speed with which they reacted. We had just moved into the new house and desperately needed furniture. A one-off grant meant I could get a couch and dining table and replace the old carpets and curtains. It certainly wasn't a palace, but it was safe. The grant was followed up with a package of financial support giving me around £80 a month. It sounds like a small sum, but it made a huge difference to our lives.

It's hard to quantify what poverty really means – for me it meant counting out every single penny. In the worst times, I couldn't even afford to change a light bulb. Poverty limited what I could do – it took away my freedom and affected my self-esteem. There was no chance of having any form of social life – even going to the cinema was out of my reach. It sounds selfish, but I really missed those little treats and flashes of culture. A part of my identity disappeared.

Soon after starting my new life, my father was diagnosed with cancer. On top of that, my son was hospitalised for 10 days. My car became even more important, as I lived 20 miles away from the hospital. When I thought things couldn't possibly get any worse, I was diagnosed with breast cancer.

During these tough few years, I tried not to feel like a victim but rather a victor. I got on with things, faced life-changing situations and tried to keep positive as best I could, but it was a massive blow when my father died.

People often talk about having the courage to go on but for me there was no alternative – to surrender to it meant going under and I had to keep myself together for my children's sake. There were some very low points but I gained insight and understanding and maintained my optimism for life.

Thankfully, my treatment for breast cancer was successful and I was able to think about moving on with my life and career. I trained as a counsellor, focusing on addiction counselling and helping women who have suffered mental and physical abuse. I also met a new partner, who is absolutely fabulous, and we have started a business together so I no longer need financial support.

Life is better now, and I have a gained so much awareness through my journey. I have a deep gratitude for all the help I received. I hope I can now make a difference to other people who may find themselves in difficult times.

# Burt Kwouk

# "Life is a series of challenges. Some you overcome; some you don't."

**Burt Kwouk's long career has spanned film, theatre and television. He's appeared in three Bond films and famously starred as Cato – Inspector Clouseau's manservant – alongside Peter Sellers in the hugely successful Pink Panther films. He was a frequent guest star on *The Harry Hill Show* throughout the 1990s and is currently a regular on our screens in the world's longest running sitcom, *Last Of The Summer Wine*.**

Life is a series of challenges. Some you overcome; some you don't. Take me for instance. My life was pretty much mapped out for me before I was born, but how different it ended up!

I came from a very wealthy family which had been successful in the textile industry. In fact, I was born in Manchester as my father was doing some research into building a factory – but we returned to Shanghai when I was a year old. When I reached 17, it was decided that I would go to university in the USA. Studying held little interest for me – I mainly concentrated on learning how to drink beer, party and smoke cigarettes.

 Burt Kwouk

The plan was that I would return to Shanghai when my studies were over and my family would 'find me something to do'. In reality, I wouldn't have to do much at all.

However, history intervened and the Chinese Communist War meant all my family's money disappeared and it was time for me to find a job. It didn't feel frightening at the time – I suppose that's the excitement and courage of youth. Maybe it was arrogance, although I prefer the word confidence. It seemed as if the world had opened up and life became a big adventure.

I drifted to Britain and worked as a hospital porter and department store assistant, occasionally supplementing my income with some film extra work. At one studio, I was picked out to do a screen test and, happily, I got the job and decided to be an actor. People laughed at me, and who could blame them? How much work could there be for a Chinese actor in 1950s London? It's not like it is today. Plus, I'd never had any acting training – in fact, I'm not trained for anything. But I decided to try it and see how it went. If I win, I win and if I don't, I'll find something else to do. I believe success is 95 per cent luck and I've always been very lucky.

There's no denying that some of the doubters were right. The way I look has been a double edged sword throughout my career. However, the lack of Chinese actors worked in my favour and meant that I could play anyone from the Far East. My look has also allowed me to play goodies, baddies and comedy roles.

At first, there was a lot of worry about how I was going to pay the bills, but my career became a series of steps and I won little breaks along the way. My first film was *The Inn Of The Sixth Happiness* with Ingrid Bergman. She was the first major movie star I came to know and she was a wonderful lady, so kind. By the time I came to real prominence in the 1970s with The Pink Panther films, I had several movie roles under my belt and it wasn't quite as rare to see an Eastern face in a film.

I am incredibly lucky – I've had a very long career and have been allowed to diversify into lots of different areas. Yes, there have been times of adversity, but it's difficult to think of anything that's been such a brick wall that I haven't been able to overcome it. I have enough confidence in my own ability, capacity or luck to get over the hurdles.

My life, like anybody's really, is a succession of problems to be solved. Sometimes I solve them, sometimes I don't. If I don't, I just have to live with it.

## Michael Aspel

# "I was an evacuee for four and a half years, and left to my own devices by the old couple who had taken me in. It was the cinema in Somerset that saved me. I used to go all the time."

Michael Aspel, broadcaster and writer, began his career as a radio actor with the BBC in Cardiff in 1955. He was one of the nation's favourite newsreaders and presented *This Is Your Life* for 15 years and the *Antiques Roadshow* for eight. Michael was awarded the OBE in 1993.

I was an evacuee for four and a half years, and left to my own devices by the old couple who had taken me in. It was the cinema in Somerset that saved me. I used to go all the time. A lady with bright red spots on her cheeks used to take me, but then the American troops arrived and strangely I never saw her again. I'd go to the pictures and re-enact all the parts

with my chums. I'd obviously play the lead – Flash Gordon or Hopalong Cassidy. They'd put benches in front of the front seats so you were staring up vertically at the screen, with your neck at 90 degrees, but it took me away from thoughts of home.

I did my National Service in Germany. To get in with the lads – because I'd been a failed officer, the most hated thing in the army – I'd endear myself by reading bodice-rippers in an exaggerated British accent. They'd sit round in a circle like boy scouts round a fire.

# Michael Aspel

I've had physically scary moments during my broadcasting career, like when I was lowered from a helicopter on to a speeding boat in order to surprise the oldest working lifeboatman in the country for *This Is Your Life*. I hit the heaving deck and then scrambled around to the wheelhouse, wondering why I'd bothered, particularly as the hero in question wasn't impressed.

Mind you, it wasn't quite as frightening as taking over the *Antiques Roadshow* from Hugh Scully. The show was so perfect and popular; I was terrified I was going to spoil it.

We did our first telethon in 1988 and I went without sleep for 27 hours. But we raised a stunning £22 million.

By the time we did the third telethon there were rows of people opposite the studio entrance with banners and things, waving and shouting my name. I went over and it turned out they were disabled, and of a militant disposition, with banners saying "Aspel, patronising pig of the year". They said they didn't want any Telethon, they wanted their rights.

It was a bit of a shock, but I absolutely understood what they meant. We were talking about them as if they couldn't speak for themselves – as if they weren't real people with hopes and ambitions. But we raised £50 million in all.

I've balanced my professional and personal life simply by pretending my professional life doesn't exist when I'm doing the personal bit. It often takes me by surprise when people come up to me in the street.

Now I'm retired, which is not my favourite word. I draw cartoons, which I usually add on the bottom of letters. I thought I might be a cartoonist once, but that's the nearest I got to it. I'm quite cheerful about the future. I've nothing to build on, nothing to impress myself with or aim for. I spend rather a lot of time staring at the ceiling wondering what I am going to do, but the great thing is I don't have to.

I admire people who retire and immediately become busy with good works.

My son was at the Lord Mayor Treloar College for disabled kids, and I support that, as well as the Hospice in Esher, and The Children's Trust. I respond, as others do, when I am asked. I turn up at things and watch the people who do the real work and then go home.

I promised myself that I'd use this time to do the drawings and writing but I'll probably just go to the pictures – and re-enact them afterwards.

# Lynda Bellingham

# "I distinctly remember sitting in the kitchen and feeling an emotional blackness."

Lynda Bellingham has a successful stage, television and film career. Her extensive credits include roles in *Doctor Who, All Creatures Great and Small, At Home with the Braithwaites, The Bill* and her series *Faith in the Future*, which won the British Comedy Award in 1997. She is still remembered as an icon of motherhood in the Oxo family ads which ran for 16 years. Recently she has appeared in the stage version of *Calendar Girls*, and as a presenter on *Loose Women*.

It was April 6th 1996 when everything just seemed to stop.

My marriage broke up, which hit me very hard – not only because it was my second marriage but also because we had children together. We had been married for 16 years. It had been a very tempestuous marriage during which I experienced physical and mental abuse – but I'd hung on in there. I really thought that if I gave it 100 per cent, it would come through.

Just as my marriage was ending, my work also fell to pieces. I was approaching that desert – 50 years old – which, as an

# 🫖 Lynda Bellingham

actress, is when it all just stops. We're not good about age in this country: at 50, you're considered an "old lady". You're supposed to go away and hide and come back later as Miss Marple.

It all seemed to happen at once. I lost my agent. I had been doing a series called *Faith in the Future* which was cut even though it had won a Best Comedy award. And then I discovered that they weren't going to do any more Oxo commercials. We'd been doing them for 16 years and although you try not to rely on these things financially, you do.

I distinctly remember sitting in the kitchen and feeling an emotional blackness.

What kept me going through this period were my children. I had to be there for them, to support them and keep up the normalities of life. One of my boys was nine years old and the other was 13, so it was the most expensive part of their upbringing! To me, it was just a question of survival. I was desperate – but I knew I just had to get on with it.

Towards the end of 1996, I got an amazing job in a film called *The Romanovs*. So, off I went to a country where nobody knew me, nobody had any preconceived ideas about me and nobody recognised me from the Oxo commercials. That was a fantastic sense of liberation for me – it was like starting again. When I got back, I decided to take the bull by the horns; I just thought: "I've got to get on and get out there".

I guess it's easy to say now in retrospect, but it is a mental attitude to begin with: is the glass half empty or half full? Instead of thinking: "Oh my God, I'm coming up to 50, my life is over", you have to think: "Oh my God, I'm coming up to 50, my life is just beginning!"

It's proved to be like that ever since really. One thing I have learned is that nothing will happen unless you make it happen. You have to make the best and the most of every single thing you do.

Roy Hudd

# "My Gran brought me up from the age of seven on her old age pension."

**A famous face in showbiz for thirty five years, Roy Hudd is a natural comedy entertainer, a talented actor, playwright, sketch-writer and performer. Roy was awarded the OBE in 2003.**

My Gran brought me up from the age of seven on her old age pension, about two and a half quid, and I didn't feel deprived at all. She took me to the Croydon Empire every week she could afford it, up in the gods, which was a huge influence on my life. I'd just left school and got a job, and I suppose I must have brought home only a few weeks wages, and then she died. She'd looked after me all those years and I was so thrilled when I took those first weeks' wages home. I gave her the whole thing and she never said a word but gave me a pound back.

The thing that got me over Gran dying was going straight into National Service and sharing life with 29 other blokes in the billet. We were all in the same boat and I don't think I've had so many laughs before or since. National Service was terrific from my point of view, and a great healer – losing my Gran, but suddenly having 29 other blokes to cope with.

Then I went into showbusiness. I'd done a lot of shows in the RAF, and had joined a Boys Club just before, and used to do shows there. That's when my pal Eddie Cunningham and I started a double act. This bloke came round after the show and said, "Enjoyed it very much, boys. Would you be interested in working for Butlins?" So that was it; we'd cracked it. Then we found we'd signed contracts for being Redcoat entertainers, so we had to do our act all over the camp but also had to

# Roy Hudd

take the kids to the fair, judge the knobbly knees, referee the football matches and dance with the duff birds at the Ball.

Eddie and I did a year or so in variety before he decided he'd rather starve at home than be touring all over the country. I became a solo act. Morris Aza, my agent, made me go down to audition in Richmond for Shakespeare – because he said variety would be all over in two or three years, and he was absolutely right. And I think that extended my career like crazy. I've always enjoyed Shakespeare.

Ned Sherrin saw me in music hall and asked if I'd be interested in doing a pilot for his satire show, *Not So Much a Programme, More a Way of Life,* and it ran for six months live on the telly. Talk about a baptism of fire! But it was great, a huge break for me.

That led indirectly to *News Huddlines* on Radio 2. It was Simon Brett's idea, though he only had the title at that time. But if you've got a show with your name on it, you're in! I worked with Chris Emmett and Janet Brown. When Janet left, Alison Steadman took over and then June Whitfield. I did 25 years of it!

I had one very bad run. The year started brilliantly. I was going to do my first radio series, my first television series for ITV, and a brand new play. We had about three months of it and then the whole thing collapsed around my ears. I just sat there. I couldn't even get a Sunday concert. It was murder. That was the worst time I ever had. I was out of work for about nine months.

I worried a lot because we had a house and a mortgage, and God knows what. I spent the time tidying up lots of things. And put my collection of songs together, which has been seriously beneficial in later life. After that was all over, I knew where everything was. It was Danny La Rue who saw me in a panto and booked me for his West End revue *Danny At The Palace*. Things started to get better from that moment on.

It was during a panto many years later that led to a big change in my career. One evening, before curtain up, the phone rang in the dressing room and a voice said "Hello, this is Dennis Potter here". And I said, "Course it is. This is Martin Borman. Goodbye", and I put the phone down. I thought it was a pal pulling my leg. But no. It was Dennis Potter, who called back and I did *Lipstick On Your Collar* for him, and *Karaoke*, and that was a huge change in my career.

More recently there's been Archie Shuttleworth in *Coronation Street* and suddenly I'm recognised by a load of youngsters.

I'm always trying to break new ground and last year I sang (believe it or not!) in *The Merry Widow* with the English National Opera at the London Coliseum. I followed this with the title role in *The Wizard of Oz* at the Royal Festival Hall. I love show business today as it is so unpredictable. You never know what's round the corner!

## Mark Curry

# "I watched as young children led their blind grandparents around the village and witnessed eye operations. All the time people continued to wash in the very same water which had caused these terrible diseases."

Actor and presenter Mark Curry spent four years presenting *Blue Peter* in the mid 1980s alongside Caron Keating and Yvette Fielding. Since moving on from the show, he has indulged his first love – theatre – including a six month run in the West End in *Woman in Black* and national tours of *Billy Liar,* and *Far From The Madding Crowd.* He has also presented several other TV shows; including *Change That, Record Breakers* and *Catch Phrase* and recently competed in the BBC's *Let's Dance For Comic Relief.*

Although it's perhaps the show I'm best known for, taking the job on *Blue Peter* was a frightening moment in my career. At that stage, I had come from my first job on *Junior Showtime* and was solely known as a children's TV presenter, so I was concerned about becoming typecast in that role.

My heart and soul really lay in the theatre and I was worried that the show would take over my life. However, I have absolutely no regrets about fronting *Blue Peter*, as it became a truly life changing experience.

Within two weeks of signing the contract, I was sent to Malawi in Africa for the *Blue Peter Sightsavers International Appeal*, where I lived rough with the villagers who had contracted horrific eye complaints from washing themselves in contaminated water. I watched as young children led their blind grandparents around the village and witnessed eye operations.

All the time people continued to wash in the very same water which had caused these terrible diseases. Although it was horrific at times, I had to witness it, as how else could we highlight this issue to children and the wider public without seeing it first hand?

The poverty I saw there, and on my visit to Russia, which we highlighted in the next year's *Blue Peter* campaign, was so extreme that it changed my whole outlook on life. I've been so lucky to keep working on stage and television throughout my career, but ultimately I am fortunate to have been able to witness that extreme poverty and help highlight the issue.

The children back in Britain were so moved by the images that, overnight, money started to roll in and we raised over £2 million, breaking all previous records. Even now, over 20 years later, I still think – what have I really got to complain about?

# Tea & Teardrops

**John Altman**

# "When I got the audition for EastEnders, I'd been on the dole for nine months, with my only acting work a commercial for a saving product."

John Altman burst on to our screens as 'Nasty' Nick Cotton in the first ever episode of *EastEnders* in 1985 and has played the character intermittently ever since, most recently returning to the show on Christmas Day, 2008. In between playing the 'baddie we most love to hate', John has completed several successful stints in the theatre, including playing Billy Flynn in a national tour of *Chicago – The Musical* and roles in films including *Quadrophenia*, *American Werewolf In London* and *The Birth Of The Beatles* playing George Harrison.

When I got the audition for *EastEnders*, I'd been on the dole for nine months, with my only acting work a commercial for a saving product. In between I'd worked on building sites,

driven cars for a hire firm and waited on tables, so when I got the audition I went prepared.

Although I've never lived in the East End of London I perfected the accent and even looked up an address to reel off to the producers in case they questioned my origins. In the event, they told me to go away and come back that afternoon so that the head producer could meet with me. Wandering around Shepherd's Bush Market, killing time and learning the script, I had no idea of the turn my life and career would take.

Playing Nick Cotton has opened lots of doors for me, but it's also closed quite a few. Having a recognisable face can work both ways. However, it's never stopped me indulging my passion for music. I get great joy from music and have been in rock bands and also many musicals and pantomimes. My favourite theatrical role was playing Billy Flynn in a national tour of *Chicago – The Musical*, performing in 525 shows up and down the country.

Exercise plays a huge part in my life. I ran my first London Marathon for Marie Curie Cancer Care back in 1988, but a stage injury three or four years ago left me with a chipped knee bone and a date with the surgeon's knife. They told me I'd never run again, but I was determined to prove them wrong. 20 years after my first London Marathon, I was back at the starting line and completed it in 5 hours 15 minutes, putting just an hour on my time from 1988. It was a mountain I had to climb ... and I'm proud to say I proved them all wrong.

# Tea & Teardrops

# "You can fool most other people at least some of the time but you can never fool yourself."

**Judith has worked in the charity sector for more than 35 years. She developed the charity Christmas card scheme, Cards for Good Causes, and also ran the National Fundraising Convention during its first five years. Judith is a vice president of Diabetes UK, sits on the international fundraising committee at the British Red Cross, has been a member of the Charity Commission's external monitoring working group and the Institute of Fundraising's Standards Committee, among many other activities. Judith was awarded the OBE in 1993.**

When I was just 21, I was asked by the Union-Castle Line to sail in one of their Round Africa vessels as a Female Assistant Purser, a new post which had been created to reflect the increasing use of their ships by holiday makers as opposed to those just sailing back and forth to Africa in the course of their work there.

This appointment came as a complete surprise to me; as I

had not really expected them to take note of my suggestion that they should trial such work.

However, after discussion at Board level, it was decided that I should sail for one trial voyage and "see how it went". If successful, they would then embark on finding others to fill such a role.

I hadn't even told my family that I had called into the Head Office that wet and windy February day after seeing glamorous pictures of liners sailing in sunnier climes. To say that they were flabbergasted was an understatement and they were extremely reluctant for me to take this step.

And so was the Company doctor, who felt it unsuitable in the extreme that I should be involved in such an undertaking! After doing his best but failing to remove the possibility on medical grounds, he told me that he was going to give me some advice.

He told me that during my travels I would face new situations and problems without any lode star or friends around me – and that every time my response fell below my own personal standards, I would lose an iota of self-respect, which I would never regain. After all, he said, you can fool most other people at least some of the time but you can never fool yourself.

That clear advice has guided my life ever since and in over 50 years I have often contemplated whether that wise man could have envisaged what a wonderful legacy he was giving to me. I have passed it on to many others – my own children and god-children in particular – and many colleagues throughout my working life.  It is simple but so true and well worth remembering, whatever the circumstances

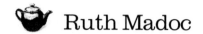 Ruth Madoc

# "Their kindness and support was amazing. It was a source of great comfort to me."

Stage and screen actress Ruth Madoc is best known for her role as Gladys Pugh in the 1980s BBC television comedy *Hi-de-Hi!* and, more recently, for her roles in *Big Top*, *Little Britain* and ITV's *Mine All Mine*. She has appeared in more than 30 pantomimes in every major city of the UK.

When John, my husband and manager, was ill a few years ago, I was hundreds of miles away appearing in pantomime in Blackpool.

John had had a hip operation and had also been diagnosed with an aneurysm of the aorta which is a life-threatening condition. He was awaiting an operation to treat the aneurysm but needed to recover from the hip surgery first.

His condition was dangerous. He couldn't move properly and had to be looked after. But I was contracted to the show and it was very difficult for me to have time off to be with him. You can imagine the worry and stress this caused. My heart was in my mouth during those months in panto.

Thankfully, we live in a wonderful little place in south Wales. A former mining village, which nestles beneath beautiful

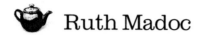 

mountain scenery at the head of the Neath Valley.

It has all the things you might imagine Welsh village life to have – a busy high street, a 'Cop' (as we Welsh call the Co-op), a rugby club, parks and the warmest community spirit you will find. It's like stepping back in time, and all the better for that. We've made so many friends since moving here from Cambridgeshire seven years ago.

We have a particular group of friends who were fantastic during the time John was poorly. Day in day out, people would pop in to see him, making sure he was OK, bringing him meals, running errands and attending to his needs.

I'd be ringing home every day to discover that John had had three of four groups of visitors. He was never short of company and support. I'd speak to my friends and they'd say, "Don't worry, Ruth, everything's under control. We'll make sure that John's looked after."

Their kindness and support was amazing. It was a source of great comfort to me and helped me get through the panto season knowing that John was in good hands. We are eternally grateful to them.

Glynneath is one of the friendliest places I know. I'll go out to buy a loaf of bread and it will take me hours before I get home because I'll be stopping and speaking to so many people en route. John is originally from Nottingham and used to city life but wouldn't live anywhere else now. He adores it here.

John, my two grown-up children and three grand-children

(with a fourth on the way) are so important to me. We are a very close family and have helped each other through hard times.

I'm an only child and when my parents died within weeks of each other, I felt like an orphan. John and my children were incredibly supportive. John is from a large family but understood my predicament. He is such an understanding man and was like a crutch to me during that difficult period we must all face.

But when people pass away, I never feel that they are really gone. I still 'talk' to my parents and my late grandmother and feel they are with me all the time.

The same goes for the friends I've lost. I've known quite a few people in show business who died prematurely, people like the lovely Simon Cadell, my co-star in *Hi-de-Hi*. Simon was a great comedy actor and was only 45 when he was taken by cancer. But he's still with me and I still have a chat with him from time to time.

## Rebecca Adlington

# "I didn't swim for two months. Being sick and not being able to swim adversely affected my training."

**Rebecca Adlington is Britain's most successful Olympic swimmer in 100 years. She won two historic gold medals at the 2008 Olympic Games, breaking a 19 year old world record in the 800m event. She is Britain's first Olympic swimming champion since 1988 and the first British swimmer to win two Olympic gold medals since 1908. Rebecca was awarded the OBE in 2009.**

In early 2005, I contracted glandular fever. It took a while to be diagnosed because I didn't realise I was sick. At first, I thought I was just tired, but after a while I thought to myself: "I can't be this tired *all* the time!" So I took myself to the doctor, where I was diagnosed with Post-Viral Fatigue Syndrome.

It was a tough time because I was in my final year of my GCSEs and I was also in training for the 2006 Commonwealth Games. Then, my sister became very ill and was admitted to Intensive Care. At first, the doctors thought she had

# 🫖 Rebecca Adlington

Meningitis, but later she was diagnosed with Encephalitis, which is an inflammation of the brain.

I didn't swim for two months. Being sick and not being able to swim adversely affected my training and, as a result, I missed out on being selected to represent England at the Commonwealth Games. It was really disheartening. In 2004, I had missed qualifying for the Olympic Games by just two seconds. It's disappointing to be so close to being able to compete and then to just miss out.

I guess a lot of swimmers would have just given up. But I knew I was a better swimmer than that. I was absolutely determined to compete at the 2008 Olympic Games and to win a medal. I had to keep my confidence up so I just kept pushing myself. That year, I competed at the National Games in the 800m Freestyle event – if I had been in the same race at the Commonwealth Games, I would have won a medal.

My coach, Bill Furniss, and my family really got me through this period. Bill kept me swimming, easing me back into training and slowly building up my schedule so that I wouldn't burn out. My parents knew how dedicated I was to swimming so they let me drop out of my A Levels. Not many parents would let their children do that, but they just said: "If you want to concentrate on your swimming, let's get you better."

They knew that my passion was swimming and that in order to be successful as a swimmer, I had to focus solely on the sport. For that, I am truly grateful.

# Tea & Teardrops

### Kate Adie

# "I've always been staggered by the number of strangers who have come to help."

**Kate Adie is the presenter of BBC Radio 4's flagship programme, *From Our Own Correspondent*. Formerly the BBC's Chief News Correspondent, she was named twice as the Royal Television Society Reporter of the Year and won the premier news award, The Monte Carlo International Golden Nymph Award, in 1981 and 1990. Kate was awarded the OBE in 1993.**

When I joined the BBC, in local radio, I had no thoughts or desires of doing news, or being a reporter. I was the most junior person on the team, on £920 per year, nailing down the floorboards and feeding the station cat. I never opted to go and lie in a ditch and be shot at. Later, as a general reporter, you just took every story that was thrown at you – quite literally sometimes. Even in small disturbances you got stones, bricks, that sort of thing. And it's horrible having gravel thrown at you, I can tell you.

In random violence people are both angry and sometimes

distraught – in a sense out of their minds with outrage, and often for very good cause; people would do anything because they were desperate. And if you get in the way, which is what the press often do, you just have to look out for yourself. Sometimes people become vindictive and you have to be very nippy on your feet. I used to be able to jump fences extremely well, and run. You're not there to take part in the fight, so if it means scarpering fast to prevent more trouble happening, you do.

This book is about facing up to danger – but about others, not me. I've been blessed and I've come through life amazed at how good it has been to me. I was born illegitimate, and I got the most wonderful adoptive parents. At the time when they slipped away, at a very dramatic and physically quite strenuous time, I was in between events in China in Tiananmen Square, and the Gulf War. Then I took the decision, and it was very quickly fulfilled, to find my own mother, and it worked out wonderfully.

Can you imagine? Thinking at one point, "I have almost no close living relatives", and then finding a tribe of them. I am acutely conscious, because a lot of people have written to me about their own experiences, that some people don't have such great good fortune. You hear from people who feel their life has been blighted. People who suddenly hit hard times, or thought things were going to be all right, and then it was not a fairytale ending and life has been very empty or bleak for them. I have been very, very fortunate.

It is terribly difficult for people who've been the victim of unexpected circumstances or tragedies, but I think you have to look into yourself and say 'It starts here - in me.' It's a tough message but people do respond. You have to gather yourself together. It helps to have friends and I'm curious when people say that if they really got into trouble they would maybe have one or two people to talk to. I would like to think I have a lot. I'm constantly nattering with them and they, as well as your family, get you through. One of the ways you gather yourself together is to call on friends. That is what friends are for. And strangers can help, too.

I've been in lots of very nasty situations where other people, not usually because of hatred of you, have occasionally tried to harm you or kill you because of the circumstances. And I've always been staggered by the number of strangers who have come to help. That's why I called my autobiography *The Kindness of Strangers*.

I've found a lot of goodness and I regard it as something very powerful in life. I don't believe everyone is perfect, or that there are saints out there. I'm not a Pollyanna. But I do think people are extraordinary, especially at bad times. I've seen amazing efforts of people giving help when they've got nothing, when they themselves have been struck by the effects of war or natural disaster. Their first thought is to go off and do something for their neighbour.

# Credits

**Interviews**

All interviews conducted by:

Huw Rossiter

Julia Shipston

Kellie Smith

Lindsey Morgan

Olivia Silverwood

Rob Tolan

Sandra Chalmers

**Photograhy**

All photographs taken by Rebecca Ward
(www.rebeccawardphotography.com)

except:

page 8      Adam Pensotti
page 12    Dwayne Senior
page 28    James Darnbrough
page 80    Christina Draper
page 112  Huw John

**Book design**

Warm Red Communications
(www.warmredcommunications.com)

Elizabeth Finn Care is a
registered charity no 207812

Lightning Source UK Ltd.
Milton Keynes UK
31 January 2010
149344UK00001B/26/P